DINOSAUR FACT DIG

CARNOTAURUS AND OTHER ODD MEAT-EATERS

THE NEED-TO-KNOW FACTS

BY
JANET RIEHECKY

Consultant: Mathew J. Wedel, PhD
Associate Professor
Western University of Health Services

Raintree is an imprint of Capstone Global Library Limited, a company incorporated in England and Wales having its registered office at 264 Banbury Road, Oxford, OX2 7DY – Registered company number: 6695582

www.raintree.co.uk
myorders@raintree.co.uk

EDITORIAL CREDITS
Michelle Hasselius, editor; Kazuko Collins, designer; Wanda Winch, media researcher; Gene Bentdahl, production specialist

ISBN 978 1 474 7 2823 2 (hardback)
20 19 18 17 16
10 9 8 7 6 5 4 3 2 1

ISBN 978 1 474 7 2827 0 (paperback)
21 20 19 18 17
10 9 8 7 6 5 4 3 2 1

British Library Cataloguing in Publication Data
A full catalogue record for this book is available from the British Library.

ACKNOWLEDGEMENTS
All images by Jon Hughes except: MapArt (maps), Shutterstock: Elena Elisseeva, green gingko leaf, Jiang Hongyan, yellow gingko leaf, Taigi, paper background

We would like to thank Dr Mathew J. Wedel for his invaluable help in the preparation of this book.

Printed and bound in China.

CONTENTS

Carnotaurus and other odd meat-eaters were hunters that had sharp teeth, keen eyesight and good senses of smell. They walked on two legs. Their arms were much shorter than their legs. They walked or ran with their stiff tails straight out behind them to keep their balance.

Some dinosaurs were very large, such as Carnotaurus. Others were small, such as Shuvuuia. Read on to learn more about Carnotaurus and other odd meat-eaters.

CARNOTAURUS

PRONOUNCED: KAR-no-TOR-us

NAME MEANING: meat-eating bull

TIME PERIOD LIVED: Late Cretaceous Period

LENGTH: 8 metres (26 feet)

WEIGHT: 0.9 to 3.6 metric tons
(1 to 4 tons)

TYPE OF EATER: carnivore

PHYSICAL FEATURES: two horns on
its head; sharp teeth; big claws

CARNOTAURUS' horns were
15 centimetres (5.75 inches) long.

CARNOTAURUS' arms
were even shorter than
Tyrannosaurus rex's arms.

The fossilized skin of **CARNOTAURUS** left marks on rocks around it. This showed that the dinosaur had scales all over its body.

COELOPHYSIS

PRONOUNCED: SEE-lo-FY-sis

NAME MEANING: hollow form

TIME PERIOD LIVED: Late Triassic Period

LENGTH: 2.7 metres (9 feet)

WEIGHT: 9 to 23 kilograms (20 to 50 pounds)

TYPE OF EATER: carnivore

PHYSICAL FEATURES: sharp teeth; long claws; long legs

Thousands of **COELOPHYSIS** fossils have been found at Ghost Ranch, New Mexico, USA. Scientists think these dinosaurs died in a flash flood.

Coelophysis lived in what is now the USA, in New Mexico and Arizona.
N
W
E
S
where this dinosaur lived
COELOPHYSIS is the state fossil of New Mexico, USA.
Two types of COELOPHYSIS fossils have been found. One has thick bones. The other has thin bones. Scientists think the dinosaurs with thick bones were males. The dinosaurs with thin bones were females.

DAHALOKELY

PRONOUNCED: dah-HA-loo-KAY-lee

NAME MEANING: small thief

TIME PERIOD LIVED: Late Cretaceous Period

LENGTH: 2.7 to 4.3 metres (9 to 14 feet)

WEIGHT: 200 kilograms (441 pounds)

TYPE OF EATER: carnivore

PHYSICAL FEATURES: strong legs; long tail; large head

Most scientists use Latin or Greek words to name dinosaurs. But paleontologist Andrew Farke used a language from Madagascar to name **DAHALOKELY**.

Dahalokely lived on flat plains in what is now Madagascar.

When **DAHALOKELY** lived, Madagascar and India were connected.

The only **DAHALOKELY** bones found so far are parts of its ribs and backbone.

DEINOCHEIRUS

PRONOUNCED: dy-no-KY-rus

NAME MEANING: terrible hand

TIME PERIOD LIVED: Late Cretaceous Period

LENGTH: 11 metres (36 feet)

WEIGHT: 6 metric tons (6.5 tons)

TYPE OF EATER: omnivore

PHYSICAL FEATURES: long arms and legs; sail on its back

Scientists discovered **DEINOCHEIRUS'** arms and claws in 1965. The dinosaur's body wasn't discovered until 2009.

Deinocheirus lived in the forested area of what is now Mongolia.

DEINOCHEIRUS belonged to a group of ostrichlike dinosaurs. It was the largest member.

DEINOCHEIRUS swallowed stones to help it grind up tough plants. Scientists found 1,400 of these stones near the dinosaur's fossils.

DELTADROMEUS

PRONOUNCED: DELL-tah-DRO-me-us

NAME MEANING: delta runner

TIME PERIOD LIVED: middle Cretaceous Period

LENGTH: 8 metres (26 feet)

WEIGHT: 0.9 to 3.6 metric tons (1 to 4 tons)

TYPE OF EATER: carnivore

PHYSICAL FEATURES: long tail; long, slim legs; thin body

DELTADROMEUS' skull hasn't been found. This means scientists don't know what the dinosaur's head looked like.

DELTADROMEUS' long, thin legs made it one of the fastest dinosaurs that ever lived.

Deltadromeus lived in what is now Morocco.

DELTADROMEUS lived in the same area as two huge carnivores, Carcharodontosaurus and Spinosaurus.

EORAPTOR

PRONOUNCED: EE-oh-RAP-tur

NAME MEANING: dawn thief

TIME PERIOD LIVED: Late Triassic Period

LENGTH: 0.9 metres (3 feet)

WEIGHT: 9 to 23 kilograms (20 to 50 pounds)

TYPE OF EATER: omnivore

PHYSICAL FEATURES: long legs; hollow bones; small head

EORAPTOR had two kinds of teeth. It had sharp teeth for cutting. Flatter teeth helped it grind or chew.

Scientists think **EORAPTOR** was one of the earliest dinosaurs on Earth.

Eoraptor lived on a floodplain in what is now Argentina.

Only a few other types of dinosaurs lived at the same time as **EORAPTOR**.

HERRERASAURUS

PRONOUNCED: huh-RARE-uh-SAWR-us

NAME MEANING: Herrera's lizard; named after the man who discovered its fossils, Oswald Reig Victorino Herrera

TIME PERIOD LIVED: Late Triassic Period

LENGTH: 4 metres (13 feet)

WEIGHT: 227 to 454 kilograms (500 to 1,000 pounds)

TYPE OF EATER: carnivore

PHYSICAL FEATURES: strong legs; short arms; sharp claws

Only 6 per cent of the fossils found near **HERRERASAURUS** are from dinosaurs. Many other creatures lived in the area.

Herrerasaurus lived on a floodplain in what is now Argentina.

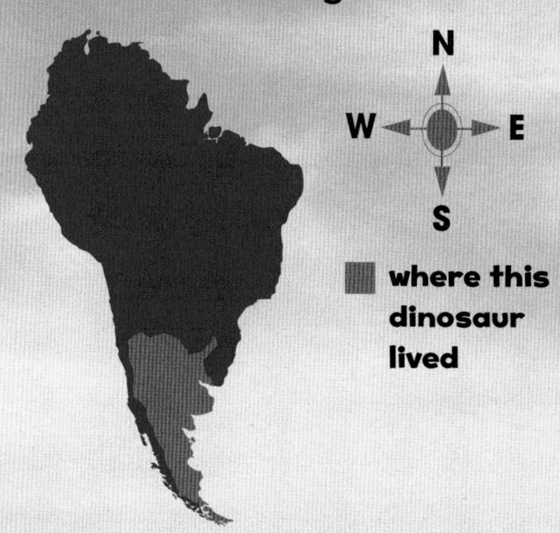

HERRERASAURUS was big. But it wasn't as big as the huge crocodile-like reptile Saurosuchus. Saurosuchus likely hunted Herrerasaurus.

HERRERASAURUS was one of the first meat-eating dinosaurs to walk on Earth.

INCISIVOSAURUS

PRONOUNCED: in-SIZE-ee-voh-SAWR-us

NAME MEANING: incisor lizard; named for its long incisor teeth in the front of its mouth

TIME PERIOD LIVED: Early Cretaceous Period

LENGTH: 0.9 metres (3 feet)

WEIGHT: 0.5 to 2.3 kilograms (1 to 5 pounds)

TYPE OF EATER: herbivore

PHYSICAL FEATURES: long legs; feathered body; long front teeth

INCISIVOSAURUS is a member of a dinosaur group called Oviraptorids.

INCISIVOSAURUS had large eyes and very good eyesight.
Only **INCISIVOSAURUS'** skull has been found.
Incisivosaurus lived in conifer forests in what is now northeastern China.
N
W
E
S
where this dinosaur lived

LILIENSTERNUS

PRONOUNCED: LIL-ee-en-STIR-nus

NAME MEANING: Lilienstern's lizard; named after amateur German paleontologist, Dr Hugo Ruhle von Lilienstern

TIME PERIOD LIVED: Late Triassic Period

LENGTH: 5.2 metres (17 feet)

WEIGHT: 91 to 227 kilograms (200 to 500 pounds)

TYPE OF EATER: carnivore

PHYSICAL FEATURES: short arms; long legs and tail; sharp claws

LILIENSTERNUS was the largest known predator of its time.

LILIENSTERNUS was a good hunter. It may also have been a scavenger.

Lilliensternus lived near rivers and lakes in what is now Germany.

Scientists only have a few pieces of **LILIENSTERNUS'** skull. Scientists think the dinosaur had a crest on its head like Dilophosaurus because their bodies were so similar.

MASIAKASAURUS

PRONOUNCED: MAS-ee-ah-ka-SAWR-us

NAME MEANING: vicious lizard

TIME PERIOD LIVED: Late Cretaceous Period

LENGTH: 1.4 to 2.3 metres (4.5 to 7.5 feet)

WEIGHT: 9 to 23 kilograms (20 to 50 pounds)

TYPE OF EATER: carnivore

PHYSICAL FEATURES: long legs and tail

MASIAKASAURUS is the only known carnivore that had teeth that bent forward.

Masiakasaurus lived in what is now Madagascar.

MASIAKASAURUS was fully grown at about 8 to 10 years old.

The scientists who found **MASIAKASAURUS** listened to music from the rock band Dire Straits. They decided to name the dinosaur Masiakasaurus knopfleri in honour of the band's lead singer, Mark Knopfler.

RUGOPS

PRONOUNCED: ROO-gops

NAME MEANING: wrinkle face

TIME PERIOD LIVED: Late Cretaceous Period

LENGTH: 6 metres (19.7 feet)

WEIGHT: 0.9 to 3.6 metric tons (1 to 4 tons)

TYPE OF EATER: carnivore

PHYSICAL FEATURES: strong legs; small, thin teeth; long tail

RUGOPS' skull is wrinkled. Most skull bones are smooth.

Rugops lived in what is now Niger in Africa.
N
W
E
S
where this dinosaur lived
Only **RUGOPS'** skull has been found so far.
RUGOPS has two rows of holes on its snout. The holes may have held a crest. It could have used this crest to attract a mate.

SHUVUUIA

PRONOUNCED: SHOO-vu-YOU-ia

NAME MEANING: Mongolian word for "bird"

TIME PERIOD LIVED: Late Cretaceous Period

LENGTH: 0.6 metres (2 feet)

WEIGHT: 0.5 to 2.3 kilograms (1 to 5 pounds)

TYPE OF EATER: omnivore

PHYSICAL FEATURES: feathered body; strong arms; long legs

SHUVUUIA lived during the same time as other small carnivores, such as Velociraptor, Saurornithoides and Gobivenator.

SHUVUUIA is the first birdlike dinosaur found with a complete skull.

SHUVUUIA had short, strong arms for digging, like a mole. It also had long, light legs for running, like a roadrunner. No creature alive today is quite like it.

YAVERLANDIA

PRONOUNCED: YAV-ur-LAN-dee-uh

NAME MEANING: named after Yaverland, where its fossils were found

TIME PERIOD LIVED: Early Cretaceous Period

LENGTH: 2.4 metres (8 feet)

WEIGHT: 50 kilograms (110 pounds)

TYPE OF EATER: omnivore

PHYSICAL FEATURES: large eyes; long feathers on arms

YAVERLANDIA probably used sight instead of smell to find food and stay away from danger. The part of its brain used for smell was small.

Only one **YAVERLANDIA** fossil has been found so far. It is from the top of the dinosaur's skull.

Yaverlandia lived in what is now the Isle of Wight in England.

YAVERLANDIA belongs to the group of dinosaurs that are the closest relatives to birds.

GLOSSARY

BACKBONE set of connected bones that run down the middle of the back; the backbone is also called the spine

CARNIVORE animal that eats only meat

CONIFER tree with cones and narrow leaves called needles

CREST flat plate of bone

CRETACEOUS PERIOD third period of the Mesozoic Era; the Cretaceous Period was from 145 to 65 million years ago

FLASH FLOOD flood that happens with little or no warning, often during periods of heavy rain

FOSSIL remains of an animal or plant from millions of years ago that have turned to rock

HERBIVORE animal that eats only plants

HOLLOW empty on the inside

OMNIVORE animal that eats both plants and animals

PALEONTOLOGIST scientist who studies fossils

PLAIN large, flat area of land with few trees

PREDATOR animal that hunts other animals for food

PRONOUNCE say a word in a certain way

SCALE small piece of hard skin

SCAVENGER animal that eats animals that are already dead

SNOUT long front part of an animal's head; the snout includes the nose, mouth and jaws

TRIASSIC PERIOD earliest period of the Mesozoic Era, when dinosaurs first appeared; the Triassic Period was from 251 to 199 million years ago

COMPREHENSION QUESTIONS

1. Why do scientists think Carnotaurus had scales all over its body?

2. Liliensternus was a hunter and scavenger. What is a scavenger?

3. How is Rugops' skull different from most dinosaur skulls?

READ MORE

Coelophysis and other Dinosaurs and Reptiles of the Upper Jurassic (Dinosaurs!), David West (Gareth Stevens Publishing, 2012)

Dinosaurs! (Knowledge Encyclopedia), DK (DK Children, 2014)

Dinosaurs in our Streets, David West (Franklin Watts, 2015)

WEBSITES

www.nhm.ac.uk/discover/dino-directory/index.html
At this Natural History Museum website you can learn more about dinosaurs through sorting them by name, country and even body shape!

www.show.me.uk/section/dinosaurs
This website has loads of fun things to do and see, including a dinosaur mask you can download and print, videos, games and Top Ten lists.

INDEX